AIRPORT MANAGEMENT AND INTERNAL SECURITY

UDOKA M. UDOKA

ISBN: 978-1-09836-4-403

ISBN eBook: 978-1-09836-4-410

DEDICATION

I dedicate this work to the Almighty God for the grace, infinite wisdom and favour granted to me in the course of undertaking this work. I ascribe to Him the glory, honour and adoration due His name, Amen

The study provided valuable roadmap to implementing the recommendations for improved airport management and internal security.

CONTENTS

ABBREVIATIONS AND ACRONYMS

CHAPTER 1

CHAPTER 2

CHAPTER 3

CHAPTER 4

CHAPTER 5

BIBLIOGRAPHY

ABBREVIATIONS AND ACRONYMS

ABBREVIATIONS

WW 1   - World War 1

CDRE   - Commodore

ACRONYMS

UK   - United Kingdom

ICAO   - International Civil Aviation Organisation

FAA   - Federal Airport Authority

SA   - South Africa

ATNS   - Air Traffic Navigation Services

SANDF   - South Africa National Defence Force

NCAA   - Nigerian Civil Aviation Authority

FG   - Federal Government

NSA   - National Security Adviser

AMA	- Airspace Management Agency
SARPs	- Standard and Recommended Procedures
MMIA	- Murtala Mohammed International Airport
MD	- Managing Director
USA	- United States of America
DG	- Director General
FAA	- Federal Aviation Authority
CAP	- Civil Aviation Policy
CCTV	- Close Circuit Television
AVSEC	- Aviation Security
IED	- Improvised Explosive Device
VIED	- Vehicle Borne Improvised Explosive Device
AHCO	- Aviation Haulage Company
GAT	- General Aviation Terminal
MET	- Meteorology
CAT	- Civil Aviation Technology
AIB	- Accident Investigation Bureau
IGR	- Internal Generated Revenue
SME	- Small and Medium Enterprise
ICT	- Information Computer Technology
NIMC	- National Identity Management Commission

e-ID	- Electronic Identity Card
ICA	- Infrastructure Concession Agency
BOT	- Build, Operate and Transfer
ASF	- Airport Security Force
ONSA	- Office National security Adviser
NSA	- National Security Adviser
NASS	- National Assembly
GDP	- Gross Domestic Product

CHAPTER 1

INTRODUCTION

BACKGROUND TO THE STUDY

1.   One of the fundamental objectives of governments worldwide is the ability to effectively manage and control their territories by land, sea and air. The invention of the aircraft by the Wright Brothers in 1903 compounded the complexities involved in the management and control of national territories. This is more so as aircraft operate from airports which need to be properly managed and protected. The success that crowned the Wright Brothers efforts on 17 December 1903 was the invention of a fully controlled self-powered, heavier-than-air machine, which was the first remarkable attempt by man to fly.[1] Subsequently, technological developments led to rapid growth in the development of aircraft, aerodrome, aviation infrastructure, and management of these assets became imperative.

2. The development of these assets gave birth to present day airport management and its economic benefits for enhanced internal security. Airport management simply refers to the processes involved in ensuring active planning, coordinating, maintaining, staffing, controlling and managing all airport activities to ensure socio-economic wellbeing, safe and efficient air operations for enhanced internal security. Internal security entails the effective control, management and protection of nation's borders. It also involves the protection of country's key and vital assets, economic, political, cultural and military strategies that would promote, preserve and maintain the interest of a nation including its citizens.

3. Globally, the effective management of airport activities in recent times has provided a viable strategy for internal security. As civil and military airport operations grew rapidly after the First World War (WW1), with aircraft flying across international boundaries under different rules and regulations, the problem of airport management and its attendant security challenges became prevalent.[2] These security challenges are referred to as accidental/malicious damage, crime, terrorism, and other security threats while methods or techniques used in an effort to protect passengers, staff, aircraft, and airport infrastructure from accidental/malicious harm, crime, terrorism, and other threats is known as airport security. The increase in air transportation necessitated the need to establish relevant bodies to coordinate the management of flights operations at the airports and ensure safety of passengers. The United Kingdom (UK), Hungary, Germany and France established regulating agencies to coordinate civil aviation requirements. An International Civil Aviation Organization

(ICAO) conference was held in 1944 to harmonize the management of civil/military aircraft operations and its attendant safety and security demands.

4.   Since its inception at Chicago Conference in 1944, the ICAO Convention, also known as Chicago Convention has been accepted by189 countries.[3] Consequently, the ICAO was established in 1947 to solve the problems associated with management of international flights. The ICAO was also tasked with the responsibility of administering universal link between all countries.[4] This is to ensure smooth management and efficient linkages among countries operating on international flight routes for enhanced internal security. The problem of providing efficient linkages between nations/countries airports to ensure safe and efficient air operations is the responsibility of airport management.

5.   In the United kingdom (UK), airport management is one of the most dynamic and rewarding sector in aviation industry in the country. The UK airport management is considered a top priority in its internal security policies since after 9/11 attacks. The UK government has taken pre-emptive measures to ensure that the countries airport management set-up is provided with conducive environment to carry out its statutory roles. This is evidenced in the scrutiny and vetting of passengers and security control checks among others at the airports for enhanced airport management and internal security in the UK.

6.   As dynamics of aviation industry increases, airport management became more and more critical to the UK's economy, commercial and security interests began to take precedence over other concerns. Thus, in UK, airport management is an established structure vested with

the responsibility of ensuring effective planning, coordinating and monitoring of the movement of people, goods and services through the airport towards achieving definite goals for enhanced internal security.[5] Increased airport activities necessitated the need to establish regulatory bodies such as Federal Aviation Authority (FAA) to coordinate flights as well as ensuring safety of passengers, crew and airport users for enhanced airport management and internal security in UK.

7.   In third world countries, taking South Africa and other developing countries as case study. Note: Third world countries have similar airport management and internal security challenges. In South Africa (SA), the Wright Brother's success story encouraged the interest of South Africa in aviation development and airport management as early as 1910.[6] South African Federal Aviation Authority manages and coordinates the activities of all agencies within the airports such as the Air Traffic Navigation Services (ATNS) among others. The ATNS is the lead agency responsible for providing air traffic and navigation services in the country for enhanced airport management and internal security in SA. Others are provincial governments, South Africa National Defence Force (SANDF) for military airports, some private organizations and individuals. The airports are partially commercialized with some restrictions to allow sustainable management of safety and cost recovery.[7] The SANDF, by constitution, managed and controlled military airports and other facilities necessary for the operation of its aircraft. This allows her the exclusive advantage of concentrating on protecting the sovereignty and integrity of the country's airspace for enhanced internal security in SA.

8.   In some developing countries, it is only recently that airport management is viewed as a sector associated with lots of economic potential by individuals, corporate groups, agencies and government and requires serious investment to keep it moving forward. In an attempt to maximize the benefit of efficient airport management, the Federal Government (FG) granted the Civil Aviation Authority (CAA) autonomy with the passing into law of the Civil Aviation Act 2006 by the National Assembly and assent of the Federal Government.[8] CAA is the regulatory body of the aviation industry. The policy thrust of the regulatory Authority is "Development of airport management of international repute for enhanced internal security.[9] Federal Airports Authority (FAA) is a service organization statutorily charged to manage all commercial airports and provide service to both passenger and cargo airlines. Generally, to create conditions for the development in the most economic and efficient manner of air transport and the services connected with it. It is in pursuant of this, that the FG would commit over Millions of Dollars to upgrade facilities and improve the management architecture of all major airports within the country for safe and efficient conduct of air operation.[10] This the government is doing to standardize the airports by regulating its policy framework in line with global best practice following the incident of 9/11 and other breaches of security at our airports.

9.   The porosity of all the country's airports is a matter of serious concern to the government and stakeholders. This has necessitated the need to improve on the existing support infrastructure and manpower to adequately man and secure this infrastructure for enhanced airport management and internal security. Others are provision of airport security network to ensure that airports are secured and safe for efficient air operations for enhanced airport management and internal security. In order to achieve these, there is the need for the government and other stakeholders to provide adequate funding to ensure that all necessary structures in line with global best practice are provided for enhanced airport management and internal security.

10.   Despite these efforts by the government, some problems still persist, hence the need for this study. Some of these problems include inadequate policy to meet the contemporary security challenges and infrastructure deficiency for safe and secure airports. Others are insufficient skilled manpower to control and manage the activities at the airports for enhanced airport management and internal security. The absence of dedicated airport security force to man the entry and exit points to identify early intrusion pose a potential threat to airport management and internal security. Realizing airport management's inherent potential, the government would conceive the vision to develop and promote airport management for enhanced internal security. In spite of these strides and aspirations, airport management would still remains plagued with paucity of funds for the provision of aviation priority equipment and infrastructure among others which undermines airport management and internal security. The purpose of this study therefore is to explore ways of improving airport management for enhanced internal security. The researcher is motivated by the desire to ensure that airports are well protected and managed to ensure safe and efficient conduct of air operations as well as guarantee socio-economic well-being of the people through enhanced airport management for internal security.

STATEMENT OF THE PROBLEM

11.   Developing countries over the years since independence have witnessed a commendable improvement in airport management in the areas of provision of associated airport infrastructure and remodeling of terminal buildings in the sector. Despite the aviation sector's enormous economic potential and the government's commitment to improve airport management, the effects on internal security are yet to be fully harnessed. Some of these shortcomings are attributable to high level of insecurity at the airport occasioned by incessant attacks by armed robbers, drug trafficking, illegal trespassing within the airport due to porous fencing, money laundering, smuggling of small arms and light weapons across the airports and recently terror threats.[11] Certainly, these are not indices of good airport management. There are thus indications that the improvement in airport management is yet to translate to the envisaged improvement in internal security. It is in view of this, that the study seeks to examine how airport management can be improved upon to enhanced internal security. Consequently, this study seeks to answer the following questions:

a.   What is the relationship between airport management and internal security?

b.   What are the issues involved in airport management and internal security?

c.   What are the contributions of airport management to internal security?

d.   What are the challenges militating against airport management and internal security?

e. What are the prospects for improving airport management for enhanced internal security?

f. What strategies could be proffered to mitigate the challenges to airport management in order to enhance internal security?

OBJECTIVE OF THE STUDY

12. The main objective of this study is to assess airport management with a view to enhancing internal security in the developed/developing countries. The specific objectives are:

a. a.Establish the relationship between airport management and internal security.

b. b.Identify the issues involved in airport management and internal security.

c. c.Examine the contributions of airport management to internal security.

d. d.Identify the challenges militating against airport management and internal security.

e. e.Highlight the prospects of improving airport management for enhanced internal security.

f. f. Proffer strategies to mitigate the challenges militating against airport management in order to enhance internal security.

SIGNIFICANCE OF THE STUDY

13. The outcome of this study will benefit policy makers, organizations, researchers and the academia. Prospective beneficiaries among policy makers are the Office of the National Security Adviser (NSA), Federal Ministry of Aviation, and the Ministry of Defence among others. This work would provide these stakeholders with strategies to consider in their effort to enhance internal security. Other organizations that could benefit include the FAA, CAA, and other relevant players in the industry. The research findings could serve as reference material for researchers as well as stimulate further research interest on the subject. The research will also contribute to the academia and the general public by extending the frontiers of knowledge on the topic. It would stimulate and aid further studies by scholars, students, policy makers and technocrats on airport management and internal security. Finally, it would also add to the body of knowledge on airport management in areas of developing policies for internal security.

SCOPE OF THE STUDY

14. Firstly, the study will focus on the period between 2015 to Dec 2020. This period is chosen because it would mark the period that the Ministry of Aviation would renew its resolve to put in place safe and efficient airport management in compliance with ICAO Standard and Recommended Procedures (SARPs) in order to enhance internal security in the face of global security challenges.

15. Secondly, this study will dwell mainly on the airport management and internal security. This is because of the nature and urgency of contemporary security challenges. Thirdly, this research work on airport management and internal security will be delimited to some airports in the developing countries due to the sheer volume of treating all airports in the third world countries and the need for a more focused and result oriented research. There are airports that are operated by FAA out of which some are international airports. In addition, there are airstrips or airfields scattered around and within developing countries, built mainly by the military and multinational oil companies. Additionally, intricately linked to operations, is the history of airports, however, the historical evolution of the various airports will not be covered.

METHODOLOGY OF THE STUDY

16. The study was a descriptive research. It employed the field survey method by the use of questionnaire and interviews to obtain data and information from samples representing the population of the study. The choice of survey method was informed by the need to collect data from a representative sample of stakeholders in the field of study. The methodology would address 6 requirements. These are the type of research, sources of data, methods of data collection, sampling technique, methods of data analysis and lastly method of data presentation.

17. **Type of Research**. The type of research undertaken was defined by the objective and level of the research, and the research design. [12] Firstly, data was collected from an integration of both qualitative and quantitative methods. Secondly, being within the realm of internal security, descriptive survey research was considered apt for the study. Lastly, the study used field survey design.

18.   **Sources of Data.**Data for the study were obtained from both primary and secondary sources as follows:

a.   **Primary Sources of Data**. The primary data were drawn mainly from experts in the field of study. The experts were drawn from Government agencies and the private sectors, and those who have been in the industry long enough to volunteer both professional and expert opinions. Primary data were obtained using questionnaires and unstructured interviews. The focus groups were policy makers, stakeholders, members of the public, organized private and informal sectors involved in the aviation sector as well as NGOs. A Copy of the Questionnaire is at **Appendix** 1. The questionnaires were distributed to the targeted personalities by hand and interviewed simultaneously. Other questionnaires were also distributed to the sample of the population to answer and return accordingly.

b.   **Secondary Sources of Data**. Secondary data were sourced from books, journals, newspapers, magazines, published and unpublished material on aviation industries and airport security from libraries, archives and internet and other sources. Some secondary data were sourced from the British Council, the United State of America (USA) information service among others. The list of secondary sources of data is at **Appendix** 2.

19.   **Method of Data Collection.**Primary and secondary data were collected through field methods and document analysis respectively. These are highlighted subsequently:

a. **Field Method.** The field study method was adopted. Primary data were obtained through unstructured interviews and use of questionnaires. The unstructured interviews were conducted through visits, telephone calls and emails while the questionnaires (close and open-ended) were administered by the researcher. See Enclosure 1 for the distribution strategy. While 20 high value persons were interviewed, the 100 questionnaires administered had a return rate of 50 per cent. The high return rate and the specialized sample size of population facilitated valid generalization.

b. **Document Analysis**. Secondary data were collected from books, journals, periodicals and newspapers. Others were through unpublished materials and the Internet. These were subjected to archival library search technique and document analysis.

20. **Sampling Technique.** The sample population of this study comprised of various stakeholders in the aviation sector as well as organized public and private individuals. The diverse nature of the stakeholders made definition of the actual population difficult. However, senior airport management staff, organized private and informal sectors involved in airport management as well as airline operators were the main focus of the interview. Nevertheless, the subjects of the population have defined characteristics; players in the aviation industry. Consequently, purposive (also commonly known as judgemental sampling) non-probabilistic sampling technique was used for this study. This allowed deliberate selection of the targeted sample based on the objectives of the research.

21. **Method of Data Analysis.** The data collected were analysed qualitatively and descriptively. In the qualitative method of data analysis, logical reasoning was applied based on facts obtained to arrive at appropriate deductions. From the outcome of the analysis, strategies were adopted to achieve the desired objectives.

22. **Method of Data Presentation.** The data generated were presented in forms of tables, charts and maps where appropriate.

LIMITATIONS OF THE STUDY

23. The inherent weakness of purposive sampling is that it does not provide for vast array of statistical procedures. [13] However, since sampling for proportionality was not the main concern of the study, the work remains valid. One other limitations of this study was difficulty in having access to a few individuals billed for unstructured interviews. Furthermore, some government functionaries in the ministry of aviation and airlines (specifically, those of the financial department) were not too forthcoming with statistics on revenue accruing exclusively from airport management and current expenditure on development of airports. These drawbacks were addressed by reliance on secondary sources and interviews with other airport functionaries.

24. It was observed that the informal sector did not maintain appropriate records on their revenue generation. This lack of data also made it difficult to ascertain the change in revenue earnings in terms of figure, since revamping of the aviation industry in some selected airports. However, to address some of these shortcomings, secondary data were utilized to fill the gap in other to achieve the objectives of the research, thus, the quality and validity of the study were not affected.

<u>NOTES</u>

CHAPTER 2

LITERATURE REVIEW

25. This chapter conceptualizes the key variables of the study and reviews some relevant literature to identify existing gap which the research intends to fill. Furthermore, a theoretical framework is presented to give a proper understanding of the theory upon which the study is anchored. Finally, examples from United States are presented on how airport management could be structured to contribute meaningfully to internal security with a view to drawing lessons for the developing countries.

CONCEPTUAL DISCOURSE

26. The key variables in this study are airport management and internal security. In this section, these variables are conceptualized and the relationship between them established.

AIRPORT MANAGEMENT

27.   Airport management according to Abdulsalam Ibrahim refers to an established structure responsible for utilization and coordination of human and other resources at the airport towards definite goals.[14] This concept does not specifically state how the airport should be organized and safe guarded and who should do it to ensure socio-economic well-being of the people. Although, it mentioned coordination which is fundamental to airport management, it did not specify what is to be coordinated and the end state. It is therefore not suitable for this study.

28.   Avjobs Airport Management Career sees airport management as the activities to ensure safe and efficient operation of an airport on a daily basis.[15] While this view captured the activities that are undertaken to ensure safe and efficient airport operations, it did not state clearly the processes of achieving the organization's goals. Thus, it is not suitable for this study.

29.   Airport management definition-answers.com refers to airport management as functions performed by someone to manage an airport and keep it running smoothly and correctly. They posit that airport management could be defined as the processes involved in bringing together specific functions of personnel, equipment, information system, and organization to ensure safe and efficient air operations.[16] This definition is not explicit enough because each of these different components has sub-divisions that require proper coordination for the achievement of organization's objectives which was not clearly brought out therefore, it is not apt for this study.

30. Synthesizing from the above definitions, the researcher conceptualizes airport management to mean the processes of planning, organizing, directing, controlling and coordinating the security and wellbeing of passengers, airport workers/staff as well as security and efficient utilization of infrastructure and facilities in the airport. Thus, guaranteeing safe air operations as well as ensure security and socio -economic wellbeing of the citizens. This overarching operational concept succinctly captures the people's interest, states the underlying motive in the systematic accomplishment which are planning, organizing, staffing, directing, security and controlling of air operations to achieve its defined objectives and benefits that it offers. It is thus considered apt for this study.

INTERNAL SECURITY

31. Internal Security is considered by some academics as a dynamic phenomenon and a persistent social problem in any society. This Phenomenon is tied to survival, stability, growth and development of any country.[17] Academics have differed on whether it is all about freedom from threats to core values and therefore could be protected by military force or should focus on the individual and several considerations of the international system. Thus, suggesting such security concepts as food security, economic, political, energy, human environment and other relevant considerations as critical references in the discourse of Internal Security are not considered here and therefore not adopted.

32. Lippman sees internal security as "the ability of a nation to maintain its core values and avoid war and if challenged, its ability to maintain such core values by victories in war.[18] This is a militaristic perception of internal security in which nations are more concerned with protection and preservation of independence and sovereignty. The social and economic transformation of the society to usher in development necessary for peace is not considered here. It is thus not considered further.

33. Nnoli sees the concept of Internal Security as a "Cherished value associated with the physical safety of individuals, groups or nation/states, together with a similar safety of their other most cherished values.[19] Although, this definition also emphasizes more on physical security which is pragmatically not explicit enough. It also failed to articulate a comprehensive view that would accommodate other critical views and therefore not ideal for this study.

34. McNamara observes that any country that seeks to achieve internal security through adequate military security in the face of acute food shortages, energy problems, population explosion, low level of productivity and per capita income, a high rate of illiteracy, a fragile infrastructure base, inadequate and inefficient public utilities has a false sense of security.[20] McNamara postulates that:

> "In a modernizing society, security means development, security is not military forces though it may involve it, security is not military activity, though it may encompasses it, security is not military hardware, though it may include it, security is development and without development there can be no security".[21]

McNamara's definition is predicated on human security and welfare of the citizens. From the above, insecurity could arise as a result of underdevelopment.

35.   McNamara's position was aptly captured by Ogunbanwo who postulated that "Internal Security is a concept that should be applied in its broadest sense to include economic security, social security, environmental security, food security, quality of life and technological security".[22] This perception recognized not only the need for credible forces to repel aggression but also the critical need for socio-economic and political transformation to eliminate poverty and increase literacy level thus enhancing Internal Security. Consequently, Ogunbanwo's definition which aptly covers critical facts of security meets the focus of this study and is therefore adopted.

RELATIONSHIP BETWEEN AIRPORT MANAGEMENT AND INTERNAL SECURITY

36.   Airport management involves the techniques and methods use in the planning, organizing, directing, and controlling airport operations to ensure safe and efficient conduct of air activities as well as ensure security and socio-economic well-being of the people. Meeting the passengers' needs entails an interacting relationship between the airlines' staff, the aviation staff and security agencies at the airport that conglomerates that attempt to respond to these needs of passengers. The security agencies, staff and beneficiaries contribute to providing a stable and secure base for air operations. These include procedures to check smuggling which rubs the nation/country of accruable tariffs and has negative economic and security implications which ultimately impinge on internal security.

37. On the other hand, Internal Security is viewed as strategy employed to combating activities that seek to undermine the socio-economic well-being and quality of life of the citizens. This it achieves by creating a conducive and secure environment for planning, organizing, directing and controlling of air and ground operations. Good airport management creates enabling environment for jobs, improves socio-economic well-being of the people and contributes to revenue generation for enhance internal security. From the foregoing, while internal security is an end, airport management is one of the means to attaining it. Indeed, effective airport management reinforces internal security. The more efficient and effective airport management is, the greater will be the internal security. The converse also holds true, other things being equal. There is therefore a direct and positive relationship between airport management and internal security.

REVIEW OF EXISTING LITERATURE

38. Some previous studies have been conducted on airport management and internal security. Viewing it from global perspective, Jenkins in his book "Airport Raises Border Issues" provided a fairly comprehensive treatment of airport management with its variants and the impact on air operations. He provided an insight into the complexities that exist in the interaction between passengers, security agencies and airport authorities. He posited that management conflicts emanate from over bearing passengers, and that these conflicts arise because there is no synergy of efforts between security agencies and

staff at the airport.[23] Though cogent enough, Jenkins's preposition did not acknowledge the fact that the same management which he alluded to as being the source of conflict is indeed also as a veritable vehicle for managerial integration, understanding, diplomacy, peace and harmony at the airports. In essence, Jenkins focused mainly on the negative impact of airport management at the exclusion of establishing a nexus between airport management and numerous diplomatic and security advantages it bestows.

39. Akpan's book titled "Nigerian Aviation Industry" (The Roles of Aviation Industry in Nigeria): The role of regulatory authorities of NCAA, FAAN and the Nigerian Airspace Management Agency (NAMA)", is classic in many respects. Akpan identified the critical roles Federal Government, NCAA, FAAN, NAMA and private sectors are expected to play in aviation security before and after the 9/11. He advocated the fostering of a strong collaboration between the regulatory agencies, airlines, government at all levels and private sectors for enhance airport management and internal security.[24] Aside the apparent lack of synergy, Akpan also identified general insecurity as a challenge militating against domestic and international airports.[25] While, Akpans's work buttressed the need for strong collaboration between stakeholders and security agencies as imperative to effective airport management, he did not focus much on the economic potential of airport management. He also did not reckon with the immense spin-off multifarious economic benefits of airport management. Aside security concerns, other factors such as policy framework, infrastructure among others were not identified as challenges militating against airport management and internal security.

40.   Airport management would thrive on long-term basis provided there are significant security measures, economic and social benefits that justify investment in the sector.[26] This is the view of Bartholomew in his work, "Airport and Aviation Security." This presupposes that once these benefits are met, airport management has infinite capacity. However, airport management, like most other sectors do have a life cycle. Bartholomew did not take cognizance of the fact that irrespective of the benefits accruing there from, once there is complacence in airport management 'carrying capacity', the Law of Diminishing Return sets in. It is thus, pertinent to continually upgrade airport support infrastructure in order to guard against decline and sustainability of airport management.

41.   Drmuren former DG NCAA, in his aviation correspondent x-rayed Nigeria's Aviation Industry in his paper titled "The Roles of Regulatory Bodies in Nigeria" from 1960 – 2009 and was reviewed in 2012.[27] In retrospect, he acknowledge the growth recorded in the aviation industry which was reflected in the performance and assets of the defunct national carrier Nigeria Airways Limited which became multifaceted and profit driven and had more than 30 serviceable wide bodied airplanes in its inventory. He asserted that mismanagement and corruption were responsible for the collapse of the aviation industry which brought safety and security of aviation to its knees.[28] He mentioned that these problems culminated in embarrassing fatal crashes which most experts agreed were avoidable. He praised the autonomy granted to the NCAA and was of the opinion that the initiative could reduce the rate of accidents thereby promoting Airport Management. This work is found useful in this study. Although, the writer's work was an appraisal of aviation industry in Nigeria, with respect to aviation safety and security but did not relate it to Internal Security.

42.   Enechukwu on airport management looked at the metamorphoses that have taken place in the sector with the attendant migration from procedural control to radar based.[29] He asserts that the radar is unique and allows expeditious Search and Rescue (SAR) which promotes aviation safety and security.[30] He posits that, airport management in Nigeria is working hard to embrace new innovations in compliance with International Civil Aviation Organization (ICAO) regulations. For instance, arrangements are ongoing to migrate from terrestrial based navigation to Global Navigation Satellite System (GNSS).[31] He opted for the need to accelerate its commencement in Nigeria due to its enormous benefits to airport management. It is observed that the writer's emphasis was on safety and security of aviation but did not relate issues discussed to airport management.

43.   Amu in 2005 examined Security and Airport Management in Nigeria. His work brought out some lapses that exist in the airport management system in Nigeria that could facilitate breach of security. He was of the view that the aviation sector in Nigeria must attract special funding from the government in order to overcome the numerous challenges of airport management.[32] Bankole in 2007, dwelt extensively on aviation safety and security in Nigeria.[33] He asserts that faulty legislation, incompetent management and government interference are the major challenges facing the industry which in his opinion has led to avoidable fatal air crashes.[34] Their research findings showed that airport management positively impact on internal security, including enhancement of the people's income.[35] Taking cognizance of the relevance of airport management to internal security, the duo consequently recommended that airport activities be organized all through to comply with the approved standard and recommended procedures in Nigeria. Their work was generally on aviation security, and not particular genre of airport management. Thus, it cannot be ascertained from their submission the extent, if any, to which airport management in particular, is contributing to internal security in Nigeria.

44.   The above works have no doubt contributed appreciably to the field of study. Virtually, all of these works either focused on aviation generally, the negative impact of airport management or the pecuniary benefits of developing aviation industry. None of the works discussed sufficiently address the nexus between airport management and internal security, the challenges militating against airport management, the prospects nor proffered strategies to enhance airport management for internal security. These are the gaps that this study seeks to fill.

THEORETICAL FRAMEWORK

45.   The theoretical framework for this study is the system theory which falls within the broad class of traditional functions of management such as planning, organizing, controlling, and communication. There are a number of theories linking management to internal security that could be applied for this study. Some of the theories considered are the Herbert Spencer, Emile Durkheim, Talcolt Parsons Models, Ludwig von Bertalanffy and Keneth Boulding System Theories. However, Ludwig von Bertalanffy and Keneth Boulding System Theories were considered most appropriate as they not only relate the 2 key variables, but also provide means of ensuring a useful way of thinking about the job of management. The study was thus anchored on the Ludwig von Bertalanffy System Theory. It provides a framework for visualizing internal and external environment factors as an integral whole. It allows recognition of the proper place and functions of sub-systems. The System within which organizations must operate is necessarily complex. However, management via system concepts fosters a way of thinking which on the other hand, helps to dissolve some of the complexity and, on the other hand helps the management recognize the nature of the complex problem.

46. Bertalanffy (1951) and Boulding (1956) propounded a modern foundation of general system theory. They build on that foundation in applying general systems theories to management. Bertalanffy asserted that structural functionalism theory, unlike most other theories focuses on the functions performed by an institution to ensure systems maintenance and survival while system theory focuses on the continuous interaction to ensure the functioning of the whole system. Organization is thus made up of interdependent sections or units which work together to fulfill the functions necessary for the survival of the organization as a whole.[36] Thus, management is created to perform statutory functions to facilitate planning, coordination and security and thereby aid the smooth functioning of the organization. These theories include Systems and Functionalism Theories among others. The Functionalism Theory is focused on the functions performed by institutions, organs or units to ensure organizational survival. On the other hand, Systems Theory conceives the phenomenon or subject matter under study as a system made of inter-related parts which exist in continuous interaction to ensure the functioning of the whole system. In other words, for an organization to work efficiently, its component parts must maintain a healthy working relationship and interaction. Every component part must be functional and contributes its quota to the overall life of the organization. In this study, System Theory is applied in explaining the work.

47.   The theory is focused on the supremacy of operating inter-relationships within a system rather than the component units. The synergy of these component units is responsible for the efficiency of the whole system. However, some scholars criticized Ludwig von Bertalanffy's System Theory who came up with their own variation of the theory that could affect management of organizations.[37] Despite this, the theory remains relevant to this work; it explains management in terms of continuous interaction of various component units to ensure the functioning of the whole system. Airport management is currently within the purview of Bertalanffy's system theory. Airport Management is therefore dependent on the functional efficiency of the sub-units such as CAA and FAA among others. Efficient airport management and internal security of a country would be difficult to achieve without the dynamic integration of the sub-units. It is on this premise that the System Theory is adopted for this study.

EXAMPLE OF AIRPORT MANAGEMENT AND INTERNAL SECURITY IN THE UNITED STATES OF AMERICA

48.   There are numerous nations/countries leveraging their airport management potentials for internal security. Essentially, these nations/countries develop their airport management sector based on their perceived threats, history and traditions. These nations/countries exploit airport management for their internal security. There are

developed countries that present good models of airport management for enhanced internal security from which lessons could be drawn. One of such countries is the United States of America.

THE UNITED STATES EXAMPLE

49.   United States of America is a very rich country in both human and material resources and endowed with many cultural diversity and attraction centers for festivals and holidays. Notable among the cultural festivals are the carnivals, spring and summer holidays. During these periods, the US is greeted with many people arriving in the country for one reason or the other, while others migrate for greener pastures mostly through the airport with the attendant security challenges. This influx of people is attended to with adequate airport management through vetting, scrutiny, planning, directing and controlling passengers at the airports. At the moment, airport management in the United States is grappling with the threats posed by terrorism. Over the years, as commercial air travel expanded, airport management and aviation security evolved along with it. Until the terrorist attacks of the 11 Sep 01, airport management was a combination of laws, regulation, and resources. The program was supposed to be a system of shared and complementary responsibilities involving the government, air carriers, passengers, and airports. In theory, the Federal Aviation Authority (FAA) set the standard and guidelines, and air carriers and airports implemented them. And if the guidelines and standard were not being followed by the carriers, the FAA was mandated to enforce the existing regime. Passengers and the users of air cargo services, who were the ultimate beneficiaries of the program, paid for airport management and security through surcharges included in the price of airline tickets and cargo shipment.[38] This is the mandate outlined by FAA.

50.   Although authority might be delegated or shared (that is, a private security company might operate the security checkpoints), the ultimate responsibility for the management of airport operations, safety and security of civil aviation rested with FAA.[39] As time went on, it became clear that Congress had made a grievous error when it gave the agency the job of commercially promoting the same industry it was charged with regulating. The "Dual Mandate", as it came to be called, was, more than anything else, to define and shape the mission, goals, and actions of the FAA. Moreover, it would eventually lead the agency, at the public expense, into a position that allowed a culture of compromise to fester.

51.   In 1996, in response to the obvious long-term negative results stemming from the Dual Mandate, Congress created new legislation that eliminated some of the language from the original 1958 bill. The FAA Reauthorization Act under Tittle IV eliminated the word "promotion" and inserted in its place "assigning, maintaining, and enhancing safety and security as the highest priorities in air commerce."[40] Surely, Congress knew all wasn't well with the FAA to have made this adjustment in language. Yet, despite the change in the mission of the FAA, the dysfunctional culture remained. The airlines continued to press their interests and the FAA, for the most part, deferred.[41] Addressing these policy deficits could ensure sustainable airport management in the US.

LESSONS

52. There are a number of lessons that could be drawn from the US model for enhancing its airport management for sustainable internal security. Some of the lessons learnt include the need for developing countries to:

a. Ensure that there is adequate policy framework on airport management and internal security.

b. Offer airport users opportunity not to merely observe, but actively participate in Airport Management security awareness campaign.

c. Imbibe the international principles on airport management for promotion, safety standards and protection of airline activities.

d. Continuously improve on existing critical support infrastructure among others.

e. Set the standard and guidelines for air carriers and airports to implement.

NOTES

CHAPTER 3

APPRAISAL OF AIRPORT MANAGEMENT AND INTERNAL SECURITY

53. This chapter presents an overview of airport management and internal security, examines the issues involved and highlights the contributions of airport management to internal security before presenting the summary of findings. Thereafter, the challenges militating against airport management, prospects of airport management for enhanced internal security will be discussed.

OVERVIEW OF AIRPORT MANAGEMENT AND INTERNAL SECURITY

54. In developing countries, Civil Aviation is a child of very humble beginnings, a spin-off of the British colonial rule. But above all else, it is a product of a mere accident of history dating back to 1925.[42] As years go by, there was a dramatic evolution in the aviation industry. Today, some developing countries have airports operated by FAA, of which some are functional international airports. In addition, there are airstrips or airfields scattered around the nations/countries, built mainly by military and multinational oil companies. These airports are managed by FAA, regulated by CAA and airspace controlled and managed by Airspace Management Agency (AMA). AMA was established by the Act of Parliament No. 48 in 29 May 1999.[43] AMA is an Air Navigation Service Provider with mandate to manage the Airspace to a level consistent with the requirement of the ICAO SARPs.

55. The management of these airports across the countries has not been an easy task hence the Civil Aviation Policy (CAP) was reviewed in Apr 2013.[44] Following this enormous task, and to lessen the burden of the management of airports by a single agency, CAP encompasses institutionalizing world class safety and security standards, development of world class infrastructure, development of aerotropolis and sharing of responsibilities among others. This review spelt out responsibilities and gave autonomy to the Civil Aviation Authority (CAA) as a regulatory agency in accordance with ICAO regulations.[45] FAA charged with the responsibility of managing airports activities could did not provide adequate policy guidelines as it relates to control and management of equipment and critical infrastructure at the airports. As a result, there exist operational deficiencies of some of the critical equipment both on ground and on board the aircraft such as transponder. Consequently, some countries airlines were banned from flying into the USA and UK for non-compliance with the ICAO standard and recommended practices (SARPs).[46] This necessitated the establishment of FAA, a service organization statutorily charged to manage all commercial airports and provide service to customers.[47] It is also established to develop and profitably manage customer centric airport facilities for safe, secure and efficient carriage of passengers and goods at world class standards.

56. These agencies have not appropriately articulated all necessary policies for efficient airport management for enhanced internal security as evidenced in the breach of security and poor airport facilities. There was however, a paradigm shift aftermath of 9/11 attack in USA. The needs to review policy to ensure improved airport management become imperative. Therefore, policy frame work is an issue in airport management and internal security. There were also fatal air crashes among others that affected airport activities which were attributed to systemic failures in airport management.[48] Other areas where the agencies charged with the management of airports have not performed optimally as evidenced in the incessant trespass of airport boundaries due to infrastructure deficiencies thereby disrupting activities at the airports which has impinged negatively on airport management and internal security. Therefore, infrastructure is an issue in airport management and internal security.

57. The intelligence gathering, surveillance, checking and monitoring of movement of people in and out of airports is not yielding utmost result due to shortage of skilled manpower. The manpower available can decisively cover the entire airports for intelligence gathering and respond to any situation found to be inimical to airport management and internal security. Therefore, manpower is an issue in airport management and internal security. In furtherance to this, the armed robbery attacks at the some airport for example in March 2013 in MMIA, 9/11 attacks and stowaway incident on Arik air from Benin to Lagos among others were also classic examples of failure of airport management to provide adequate security at the airports which has negative implication to internal security. The spate of armed robbery attacks and breach of security at airports showed that airport management has failed to provide favourable environment for effective and efficient air operations for enhanced airport management and internal security. Therefore, airport security is yet another issue in airport management for enhanced internal security.

58. To further boost airport management profile, the FG released Millions dollars for airport remodeling and upgrade of existing equipment. However, funding is hampering aviation industry from developing airports to international standard. Similarly, adequate perimeter fencing mounted with CCTV cameras, building of watch towers and security equipment among others are not provided in most airports due to paucity of fund. From the foregoing, these are modest and realizable goals that could have been achieved, if factors bothering policy framework, critical support infrastructure, skilled manpower, airport security and funding among others are adequately addressed. These are issues arising from the overview of airport management and internal security. These issues are discussed subsequently.

ISSUES INVOLVED IN AIRPORT MANAGEMENT AND INTERNAL SECURITY

59. The issues involved in airport management and internal security include policy framework, support infrastructure, manpower, airport security and funding. These issues are discussed subsequently.

POLICY FRAMEWORK

60. The Civil Aviation Policy thrust is that the primary role of the government in the aviation sector shall be to provide an enabling environment for safe and efficient conduct of aircraft operations and other attendant services. It also states that government shall encourage the accessibility of air transportation to every part of the country among others.[49] However, the entire policy document did not consider the emerging contemporary security challenges. The growing contemporary security challenges in the world today are a major determinant for efficient airport management and internal security. Therefore, airport management will thrive in a well secured environment for enhanced internal security. Today, one cannot stop making reference to the incident of 11 Sep 01 that grossly undermined airport management and internal security in the USA. This singular incident by the terrorists group has changed the dynamics of security as more stringent measures are being introduced at airports to ensure efficient airport management for enhanced internal security.

61. However, looking at that the statutory right of FAA which is to manage all commercial airports and provide service to customers, no mention was made of robust security measures that will ensure the safety of passengers and airport facilities. It is against this background that a remarkable development would be the formulation of a policy that will guarantee adequate security of passengers and airport facilities for enhanced airport management and internal security. This could be promulgation of a policy for the establishment of a dedicated security force that will provide conducive environment for safe and efficient air operations for enhance airport management and internal security.

62.   Of much concern among the policy framework is the state of airport security in some countries around the world. The security at the airport cannot guarantee the safety of passengers and airport facilities should there be any armed robbery or terror attacks at the airport. Section B, Question 4 of the Questionnaire was aimed at eliciting respondents' view on extended policy on establishing a dedicated airport security in support of airport management. Of the 50 respondents, 5.2 per cent strongly agreed (SA), 6.1 per cent agreed (A), 8.2 per cent were undecided (U), 15.0 per cent disagreed (DA) and 65.5 per cent strongly disagreed (SD). The views expressed by respondents are shown in Table 3.1 and represented in a pie-chat at Figure 3.1.

Table 3.1:   Respondents' Views on State of Policy Framework in Support of Airport Management for Internal Security.

Serial	Respondent	SA	A	U	D	SD	Total	Remarks
(a)	(b)	(c)	(d)	(e)	(f)	(g)	(h)	(i)
1.	Number	3	4	4	8	33	50	
2.	Percent age	5.2%	6.1%	8.2%	15.0%	65:5%	100%	

Source: Researcher's field survey .

Figure 3.1: Pie –Chart on Respondents' Views on Sate of Policy framework in Support of Airport Management for Internal Security.

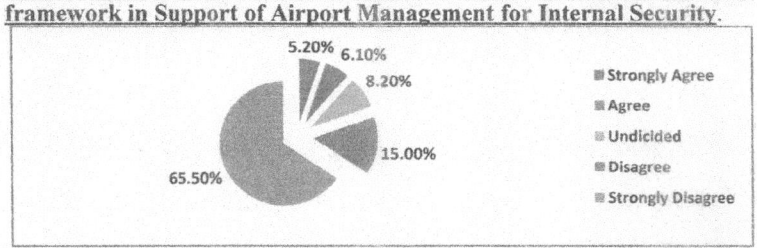

63.   From the above, a total of 41 respondents representing 80.5 per cent either strongly disagreed or disagree that the state of airport security in support of airport management is satisfactory. Therefore, this underscores policy framework as a major issue in airport management and internal security.

<u>SUPPORT INFRASTRUCTURE</u>

64.   Infrastructure is one of the fundamental issues surrounding sustainable development of airport management. Development of infrastructure is imperative to the realization of this aspiration through availability of critical support infrastructure such as watch towers at the airports. Others are barb wire fencing mounted with computer controlled electric spikes, cameras and alarm system, good road network around the perimeter fence for regular patrols day and night among others. There are some airports in some countries with average of 35.4 million passengers passing through her airports in a year.[50] Therefore, to ensure safety and security of these passengers and airport facilities adequate security infrastructure need to be put in place for enhanced airport management and internal security.

65.   To safe guard against this and ensure sustainability, it is pertinent that critical security infrastructure are continuously upgraded and improved upon to keep pace with the increasing demands of air transportation for enhanced airport management and internal security. Of much concern among the critical security infrastructure is the infrastructure deficiency of perimeter fencing and watch towers. For instance MMIA occupied a land mass of approximately 23 Km of which 80 per cent are poorly fenced.[51] Question 1, Section C of the Questionnaire was aimed at eliciting respondents' view on the state of critical security infrastructure like access roads, perimeter fence, CCTV, and watch towers in support of airport management for enhance internal security. Out of 50 respondents, 1.5 per cent strongly agree (SA), 5.0 per cent agree (A), 2.0 per cent were undecided (U) and 11.5 per cent disagreed (DA) and 80.0 per cent strongly disagreed

(SD). The views expressed by respondents as shown in Table 3.2 and represented in a pie chart at Figure 3.2.

Table 3.2 : Respondents' Views on State of Infrastructure in Support of Airport Management and Internal Security.

Serial	Respondent	SA	A	U	D	SD	Total	Remark
(a)	(b)	(c)	(d)	(e)	(f)	(g)	(h)	(i)
1.	Number	1	3	1	6	40	50	
2.	Percentage	1.5%	5.0%	2.0%	11.5%	80%	100%	

Source: Researcher's field survey, 2020.

Figure 3.2: Pie-Chart on Respondents' Views on State of Infrastructure in Support of Airport Management for Internal Security

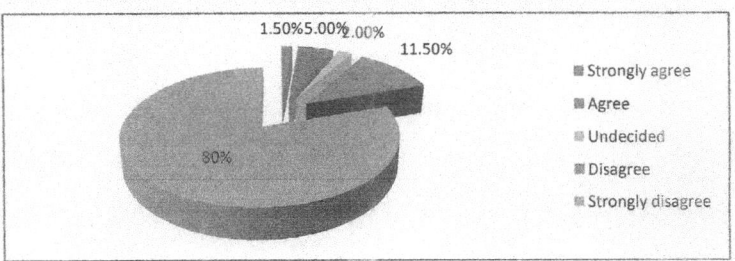

Source: Researcher's field survey, 2020.

66.   A total of 46 out of 50 respondents representing 91.5 per cent strongly disagreed or disagreed that the state of critical security infrastructure in support of airport management is satisfactory. Therefore, critical support infrastructure is a major issue in airport management and internal security.

MANPOWER

67.   Skilled manpower in security related fields that derive efficient airport management is still deficient in the aviation industry. Airports are not adequately man by trained Airport Security personnel (APS),

where unauthorized people jump or pass through broken down fences into the airport undetected. Others are the attacks by armed robbers at MMIA, Lagos at different times and cases of stowaway incidents are manifestations of inadequacy of APS personnel to observe and arrest violators for enhanced airport management and internal security.

68. Therefore, there is no substitute to trained personnel to ensure that favourable environment is provided for safe and efficient air operations for enhanced airport management and internal security. Also, considering the large number of airports in the some countries, it is expedient to have a commensurate number of skilled manpower to cater for the need of airport management for enhanced internal security. This manpower could be trained in areas of intelligence, surveillance and monitoring of the movement of people in and out of the airports to ensure possible detection of suspicious movement. Therefore, skilled manpower is still a major issue in the airport management for enhanced internal security.

69. In response to Question 5, Section B of the Questionnaire, respondents expressed their views on the level of skilled manpower in support of airport management. Of the 50 respondents, 5.6 per cent strongly agreed (SA), 21.2 per cent agreed (A), 8.8 per cent were undecided (U), 11.2 per cent disagreed (D) and 53.2 per cent strongly disagreed (SD). This views expressed by respondents are shown in Table 3.3 and represented in a pie -chart at Figure 3.3.

Table 3.3: Respondents' Views on the State of Skilled Manpower in Support of Airport Management and Internal Security.

Serial	Respondent	SA	A	U	D	SD	Total	Remarks
(a)	(b)	(c)	(d)	(e)	(f)	(g)	(h)	(i)
1.	Number	3	11	4	7	28	50	
2.	Percentage	5.6%	21.2%	8.8%	11.2%	53.2%	100%	

Source: Researcher's field survey, 2020.

Figure 3.3: Pie-Chart on Respondents' Views on the skilled Manpower in support of Airport Management and internal Security.

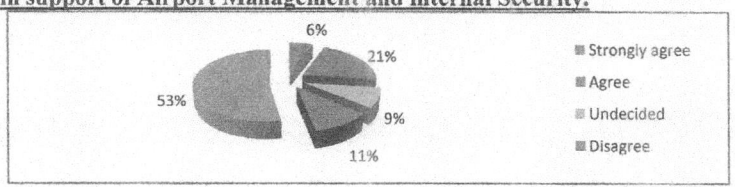

70. From the above, a total of 35 respondents representing 64.4 per cent, either strongly disagreed or disagreed that the state of skilled manpower in support of airport management is satisfactory. This view was also corroborated by stakeholders in the various departments that were interviewed. Therefore, the state of skilled manpower constitutes an issue in airport management and internal security.

AIRPORT SECURITY

71. Airport Security refers to the techniques and method used in protecting passengers, staff and aircraft which use the airports from accidental/malicious harm, crime and other threats."[52] Threats to airports security are both major and minor. [53] The minor threat may not directly threaten airline security but could develop into a major threat if unchecked. It is also a pointer to the fact that there are lapses in the security architecture around the airports. For example, armed robbery attacks at some airports and trespasses at the airports as a result

of porous and uncontrolled exits are also a pointer to the fact that there are lapses in the security set up around the airports generally. Among these minor threats are, touting, unlawful entry, hawking, drug trafficking, money laundering, pilfering of fuel and stealing.[54] These crimes have impacted negatively on airport management and internal security.

72.   The major breaches to airport security are: unauthorized accesses to aircraft, aircraft hijacking and smuggling of IEDs into aircraft, airport environment and possibility of stowaway carrying IEDs into wheel wells among others. For instance, Arik aircraft on November 2013 on a domestic flight from Benin to Lagos was found carrying a stowaway on a wheel well and successfully landed at Local Terminal of MMA2, Lagos among others. These and few others are clear indication that the tendencies for a major breach of security does exist, which are clear indications of impending threats to airport management and internal security. More so, some countries have been included on the watch list of terrorist nations by the United States after the incident of 25 December 2009, when a Nigerian departed through MMIA, Lagos and was arrested onboard a US carrier for alleged bomb attempt.[55] This had a very serious implication on airport management and internal security. Therefore, airport security is an issue in airport management and internal security.

73.   Questions in Section D of the Questionnaire were posed to obtain respondents' views on the state of security at the airports in support of airport management is satisfactory. Of the 50 respondents, 6.0 per cent strongly agreed (SA) that it was, 17.8 per cent agreed (A), 11.2 per cent were undecided (U), 16.6 per cent disagreed (D) and

48.4 percent strongly disagreed. The views expressed are tabulated and represented pictorially in Table 3.4 and Figure 3.4 respectively.

Table 3.4 and Figure 3.4 respectively.

Table 3.4: Respondents' Views on State of Security in Support of Airport Management and internal Security

Serial	Respondent	SA	A	U	D	SD	Total	Remarks
(a)	(b)	(c)	(d)	(e)	(f)	(g)	(h)	(i)
1.	Number	3	9	6	8	24	50	
2.	Percentage	6.0%	17.8%	11.2%	16.6%	48.4%	100%	

Source: Researcher's field survey, 2020.

Figure 3.4: Pie-Chart on Respondents' Views on the State of Security in Support of Airport Management and Internal Security

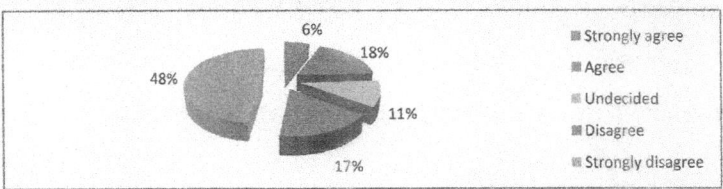

74. About 65 per cent of respondents either strongly disagreed or disagreed that the state of security in support of airport management is satisfactory. This view was also corroborated by stakeholders in the security sector that were interviewed. Therefore, the state of airport security constitutes an issue in airport management and internal security.

FUNDING

75. Funding is one of the fundamental issues surrounding sustainable implementation of airport management. Implementation of security out fits, provision of amenities and creation of safe and conducive environment for airport management to thrive is predicated on funding. It is also through funding that security equipment such as back scatter, computer controlled X-ray machines and metal and bomb detectors, infra-red mounted and camera detectors, CCTVs, building of security infrastructure among others are predicated upon. Revenue accruing to Aviation Industry from some Federal allocations are substantially insufficient to accommodate robust management and security equipment necessary to secure nation's airports for effective airport management and internal security. This development, amidst other competitive demands for funds, makes funding of airport management an issue of serious concern.

76. An analysis of budgetary allocation to Aviation Industry fiscal years in the year under review shows that actual releases have not taken cognizance of security aspect at the airports. In 2020, some huge amount of money might have been appropriated as an intervention fund to reactivate and acquire new infrastructure for active monitoring of airspace.[56] However, no consideration was made of airport security putting into account the world out-cry on ineffective security at the airports. In a year, the sum of 3 billion dollars could have been released for aviation and power sectors, no consideration was made for improved airport security, this ultimately x-rayed the importance the government has attached to airport security.[57] It is hoped that critical security infrastructure would have been adequately catered for in the budget to provide conducive environment for enhanced airport management and internal security.

77. It is thus pertinent that a well-organized airport management be established and given due consideration in budgetary allocations. Question 6 of the Questionnaire was designed to obtain respondents' views on the establishment and sufficiency of fund releases to enhance airport management in line with the global best practices. The analysis showed that a total of 70.4 per cent of respondents either strongly disagreed or disagreed that the airport management is sufficiently funded, 17.5 per cent are undecided while a total of 12.1 per cent strongly agreed or agreed. Budgetary allocation might not be in the purview of the public domain. Taking cognizance of this, some key functionaries at the MMIA such as MD FAA, AMA, CAA and Airport Managers, Ministries, Government and relevant organizations were interviewed. Their positions collaborated the views of the respondents.

Table 3.5: Respondents' Views on Funding in Support of Airport Management and internal Security

Serial	Respondent	SA	A	U	D	SD	Total	Remarks
(a)	(b)	(c)	(d)	(e)	(f)	(g)	(h)	(i)
1.	Number	4	3	9	10	25	50	
2.	Percentage	7.0%	5.1%	17.5%	24.4%	50%	100%	

Source: Researcher's field Survey, 2020.

Figure 3.5: Pie-Chart on Respondents' Views on Funding in Support of Airport Management and Internal Security

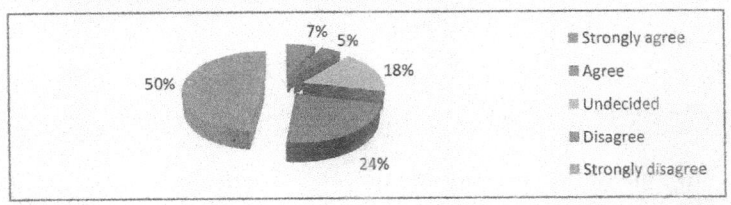

78. Going by the verdicts of respondents and the views of experts in the field of aviation, it can be deduced that airport management is not sufficiently funded. Funding therefore is an issue in airport management and internal security. The envisaged rapid economic development in some airports have not been realized thus far, nevertheless, airport management is contributing to the economic development as well as ensuring socio-economic well-being of the citizens.

The contributions of airport management to internal security are discussed subsequently.

CONTRIBUTIONS OF AIRPORT MANAGEMENT TO INTERNAL SECURITY

79. The development and enhancement of airport management is contributing to internal security in a number of ways. These contributions include increased revenue generation, growth of medium and small scale enterprises at the airport, employment generation and improved import and export businesses. There are discussed subsequently.

INCREASED REVENUE GENERATION

80. Airport management is contributing substantially to increase in revenue generation for the aviation industry, public and organized private as well as individuals who rented stalls at the airport terminal buildings. For instance, Banks at the terminal buildings are always very busy involved in one form of currency exchange to another for passengers and businessmen. As a result, most hotels, banks, restaurants, transporters, souvenir shops and petty traders experience substantial increase in their earnings during the peak periods.

81. Airport management and the airlines also make high rate of turnover during the peak periods. Specifically, the some airports witness an increase in revenue generation from a monthly average of 2.5M dollars prior to the peak periods, to 3.5M dollars to 4M dollars during summer holiday and December holidays respectively. [58] Similarly, airlines, cargo haulage companies and hotels at the airport also experience over 40 per cent increase in earnings during peak periods.[59] Similarly, some airports hosted 57.6M passengers in 4 years. This is illustrated in the Table 3.6 below. From the above, it can be deduced that increased airport activities during peak periods have positive financial contribution to the aviation industry and subsequently internal security.

Table 3. 6 Nigerian Airports Hosted 57.6M Passengers in 4 Years

Serial	Year	No Passengers	Increase Rate	Decrease Rate	Rate %	Crashes	Remarks
(a)	(b)	(c)	(d)	(e)	(f)	(g)	(h)
1.	2017	13,891,677	908,281	-	6.50	-	
2.	2018	14,899,958	908,281	-	6.50	-	
3.	2019	14,116,970	-	773,168	5.19	-	
4.	2020	14,641,768	524,978	-	3.72		

Source: www. dailytrust.com.ng

82. International airport, the commercial nerve-centre of business activities, is a beehive of activities during the festive periods. According to some Heads of Commercial Department FAA, there are over 253 shops provided at the terminal buildings alone which were fully patronized by travelers, with most of them making close to 100 per cent profit during the peak periods.[60] Similarly, transporters, airport cabs and restaurant owners interviewed, all alluded to substantial percentage increase in revenue earnings compared to the pre-peak periods. This increase in revenue earnings contributes to the economic well-being of the citizens, which is pivotal to internal security.

83. The aviation industry has the potential for revenue generation. Aside tax remittances from the above mentioned business concerns, the Civil Aviation Act 2006, saddled the Authority with the collection of 5 per cent sales charge on all tickets originating from the airports, cargo operations and charter/contract flights. The 5 per cent sales charge after collection is shared with other aviation agencies namely AMA, IMET, CAT and AIB as approved by the Civil Aviation Act 2006. This is substantiated by the steady growth in the FAA Internal Generated Revenue (IGR) since 2018 which was 33.1M dollars in 2019 it was 35.6M dollars. Specifically, the IGR for FAA rose to 36M dollars in 2020 and showed steady rise as passenger traffic increases along with 5 per cent other charges accruable to the sector.[61] A total of 104.7M dollars was generated in 3 years. FAA remitted 130M to FG. A Table 3.7 Depicting the Growth in IGR is shown in a Bar Chart below.

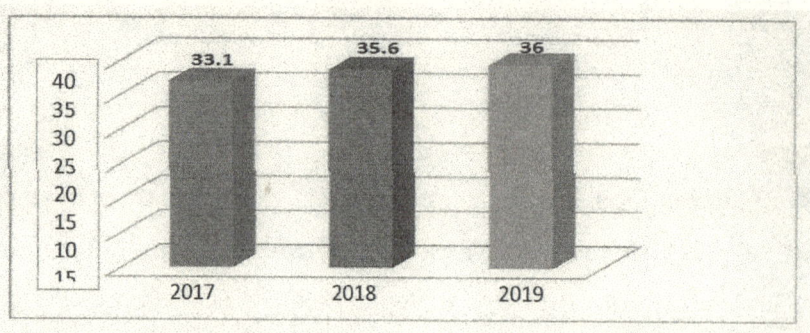

Source: www.alfrica.com

84. Therefore, the enhancement of airport management is contributing appreciably to revenue generation for the FG, aviation sector, the organized private and public sectors thereby enhancing internal security.

GROWTH IN SMALL AND MEDIUM SCALL ENTERPRISES

85. One of the indicators of internal security is providing enabling environment for businesses within the country to thrive and ensure socio -economic well-being of the people. Effective airport management provides conducive atmosphere for increase, expansion or retention of business ventures within and outside the airport terminal buildings. The number of SMEs engaged in supplying consumables and meeting passenger's needs at all times is fast growing. For instance, the re-modeling and expansion of terminal buildings in virtually all the airports would create exponential increase in number of business outlets within the airports. This is thus a significant contribution to airport management for enhanced internal security.

86.   Available records at the FAA Commercial Departmentat some airports indicate a remarkable growth in registered SMES. These are indicators of a thriving economy. The increase, expansion and retention of SMEs as avenues for wealth creation are some of the significant contributions of airport management to internal security.

EMPLOYMENT GENERATION

87.   One of the distinctive characteristics of airport management is its capacity to create jobs for teaming youths either directly or indirectly through various public and private sectors domicile within the airports. The aviation industry is a service-oriented and labour-intensive sector as opposed to use of machinery and technology in most other sectors of the economy. For instance, while a few staff could be employed to man a 50M dollars-worth ICT infrastructure, same amount invested in developing airport infrastructure would create jobs for thousands. It is therefore cheaper to create jobs in airport than most other sectors. For instance in Dubai, the terminal buildings alone are complete departmental stores and super markets busy 24 hours daily. Similarly, in Nigeria, the aviation industry is fast emerging as one of the highest employer of labour due to its series of business outlets established within the airport environment.

88. In 2013, the World Bank Aviation Employment Opportunities conducted an analysis on impact of airport management on jobs creation some countries. The findings revealed that one airport alone generated a total of 1,500 jobs.[62] Private investments that create these jobs include airlines, travel agencies, Banks, hotels, eateries, transporters, supermarkets, crafts, gifts, among others. Employment generation is thus another visible contribution of airport management to internal security.

PROMOTING IMPORT AND EXPORT BUSINESSES

89. Airport management has become one of the decent modes of the century for promoting import and export business transactions and achieving international economic exchanges.[63] It enables international business transactions among people of diverse culture and race from the most distant parts of the globe thereby improve socio-economic wellbeing of the people. Interaction between citizens and passengers which most times start from the airport arrival and departure lounges can help build business contact and common understanding between peoples.

90. The regular movement of businessmen, State and Federal Government Officials for the purposes of import and export among others from one country to another helps to promote economic development. This contributes to making the world a 'global village.' Airport management is thus helping to bridge the gaps, douse differences, fosters business integration between the travelers, business class and the rest of the world. These contributions notwithstanding, there are a number of challenges militating against airport management for enhanced internal security.

CHALLENGES MILITATING AGAINST AIRPOR T MANAGEMET FOR ENHANCED INTERNAL SECURITY

91. There are challenges militating against airport management and internal security. Some of these challenges are inadequate policy framework, infrastructure deficiency, insufficient skilled manpower, ineffective airport security and inappropriate budgetary allocation. These are discussed subsequently.

INADEQUATE POLICY FRAMEWORK

92. A major challenge to airport management is inadequate national policy on airport management and internal security. Airport management in recent times has witnessed some drawbacks as incidences of crimes at the airports tend to obstruct normal flow of airport activities. Currently, there is no adequate policy to counter incidences of criminal activities at the airports such as pilferage, theft, armed robbery, assaults and recently terror threats among others at the airports. The Civil Aviation Policy thrust is that the primary role of government in the aviation industry shall be to provide an enabling environment for growth and safe operation of aircraft and other attendant services. It also states that government shall encourage the accessibility of air transportation to every part of the country among others.[64] This policy does not adequately cover some aspects of contemporary security challenges facing airports today. Therefore, there is the need to have adequate policy in place that will guarantee safe and efficient air operations for sustainable airport management and enhanced internal security. Airport as a major component of a nation's border demands absolute policy establishing a competent security force to protect it from any criminality and possible terror attacks among others for enhanced airport management and internal security.

93. The effectiveness of security agencies at airports has been hampered by the ill-defined nature of airport security, lack of coordination among the agencies, poor state of equipment and corruption among others.[65] These agencies have also been constrained by their non-integration into the airport security and communication plan.[66] There is also the problem of lack of operational joint doctrine for airport defense in case of terrorist attack. Improving the capacities of these agencies has underscored the need for re-orientation, retraining, provisioning of modern equipment among others. These agencies need to be integrated into the airport protection/defense plan and joint operational doctrine. Integrating their communication and surveillance capabilities and converting the law enforcement agencies into a first line of defense at the airports will further enhance airport management and internal security. Thus, beside factors such as force structure, motivation and training, the strength of security agencies is inadequate to effectively secure the airports. Security is the life wire of every policy. Therefore, inadequate policy framework on airport security is a major challenge to airport management and internal security.

INFRASTRUCTURE DEFICIENCY

94. One of the main operational challenges of airport management is dearth of infrastructure. Deficiency of adequate operational, surveillance and communication equipment, CCTV, and watch towers at strategic positions at the airport perimeter fence. It engenders low morale and encourages lack of seriousness at duty posts which are critical to airport management and internal security. There are inadequate facilities for some security agencies at some airports to provide enabling environment for airport management to thrive. This creates opportunities for crimes at the airports, which have adverse implication on airport management and internal security. Dearth of infrastructure remains a serious challenge to airport management and internal security.

95. Provision of infrastructure at airport is critical to safe and efficient air operations for enhanced airport management and internal security. Therefore, there is the need for the aviation industry to impress on the government to provide critical security infrastructure at the airports to help curb the contemporary security challenges facing airports. This infrastructure such as watch towers, perimeter fence mounted with CCTV cameras, access roads, among others will be enabler for effective airport management for enhanced internal security.

INSUFFICENT SKILLED MANPOWER

96. The effectiveness of the airport management in enforcing effective control and coordination of airport activities is hampered by insufficient skilled manpower. There are problems of well-trained manpower to handle the aspects of security challenges affecting efficient airport management for enhanced internal security. Some of the areas where this manpower requires adequate training are in the operation of security vehicles for surveillance (Back scatter etc.), scanners, metal detectors, CCTV cameras, 4-wheel duty vehicles, binoculars and communication equipment. The interview conducted with some aviation security personnel revealed that some of the personnel do not know how to use and read hand held scanners. The porosity of the airports has also been blamed on airport management which has negative implication on internal security.[67] There are also no adequate surveillance equipment for the existing security agencies at the airports to have territorial domain awareness for enhanced airport management and internal security.

97.   Furthermore, considering the prevailing security challenges in some countries, there is the need for governments to recruit and train more personnel to be able to continuously monitor the influx of people in and out of the airports. These monitoring will help to identify would be terrorist or other criminal agents operating within and around the airport for enhanced airport management and internal security. Increasing numbers of airports is also increasing the vulnerable targets to criminal and terrorist alike. Therefore, it is imperative that the governments are prepared to ensure that adequate manpower is trained to ensure the security of passengers and facilities at the airport for enhanced airport management and internal security. Therefore, insufficient skilled manpower is a challenge to airport management and internal security.

INEFFECTIVE AIRPORT SECURITY

98.   Ineffective airport security is a major challenge militating against airport management for enhanced internal security. The thriving aviation industry has given rise to an upsurge in crime and other illegal

activities at the airports. Incidences of criminal activities and threats of terror attacks among others are challenges to airports management and internal security. This increase in crimes has not been adequately met with a commensurate increase in strength of security agencies required to counter it including threats of terror attacks at the airports.

99. Similarly, the high concentration of people on large airliners, the potential high death rate with attacks on aircraft, and the ability to use a hijacked airplane as a lethal weapon may provide an alluring target for terrorism. Whether the terrorists succeed or not, following the various attacks and attempts around the globe in recent years has made them serious threats to airport security. Airport security attempts to prevent any threats or potentially dangerous situations from arising or entering the country. If airport security does succeed in this, then the chances of any dangerous situations arising or illegal items entering into both, aircraft or airports are greatly reduced.[68] Airport security serves several purposes: To protect the aircraft and country from any threatening events, to reassure the travelling public that they are safe and to protect the country and their people.[69] Once these alluring goals are not met, there are chances that safe and efficient air operations will be jeopardized which ultimately hamper airport management. Therefore, ineffective airport security is a challenge to airport management and internal security.

INAPPROPRIATE BUDGETARY ALLOCATION

100. Inappropriate funding is a challenge to airport management as it affects the effectiveness of identified airport operations and addressing infrastructural deficiencies. This can be seen in deficiency of existing infrastructure and equipment such as back scatter, CCTV, security vehicles, access road among others. For instance, a personal survey of some airports revealed that they are underdeveloped and lack basic security facilities. In some countries, the government could set aside some huge amount of money for aviation and power sectors to enable it develop and put all necessary infrastructures in place at the airports.[70] Some of these infrastructures are yet to take adequate shape or installed at all to improve on the infrastructural deficit and boost airport management for enhanced internal security. The aviation sector should set for itself an aggressive development agenda aimed at reconstructing the deplorable fence and construction of some adequate security infrastructure.

The funding gaps for the construction of security fence with barb wires mounted with CCTV at all the airports and watch towers stands currently at 80 per cent.[71] Equally hampered by paucity of funds is the purchase of Back scatter vehicles and other scanning and security equipment for the airports. This is to enable airport management in the country to have good, effective and efficient service delivery devoid of security breaches. Inappropriate budgetary allocation for the construction and development of infrastructure and equipment that have direct bearing on airport operations and airport security in the aviation sector is therefore a challenge to airport management and internal security. Despite these challenges, there are some prospects for airport management to enhance internal security as discussed subsequently.

PROSPECTS OF AIRPORT MANAGEMENT AND INTERNAL SECURITY

101.   Several prospects identifiable in airport management and internal security. They include; aviation intervention fund, airport remodeling, airport expansion, national identity management commission in aviation and national carrier.

AVIATION INTERVENTION FUND

102. The Aviation Intervention Fund could be formally launched and jointly administered by the Ministry of aviation and the Federal Airports Authority. Certain recommendations could be made to assist and to ensure that the aviation sector improves. One of the recommendations is that certain huge amount of money should be released to the aviation sector in order to take care of the infrastructure deficits of the international airports. That is a specific mandate and that is a recommendation. This could be the money that would constitute the Aviation Intervention Fund.

103. The idea of the intervention fund could be conceived out of Government desire to change the status of the nation's airports to compete favorably to that obtained abroad. The Government is to, among other things, encourage, support and facilitate proper funding of the aviation sector in order to build capacity necessary for proper airport management for enhanced internal security. It is therefore expected that the intervention fund would revitalize the development of the aviation sector for the better. The approval of the aviation intervention fund is thus a prospect for airport management and internal security.

AIRPORT REMODELLING

104. Airport remodeling is a growing prospect for airport management and internal security. According to aviation expert, reports that deluge of doubts that trailed the commencement of remodeling of airports, is giving way to rays of hope for some airports projects. Government could approve the remodeling of airports especially the terminal buildings to meet international standards. The first on the list of projects to be developed is terminal buildings which have gone so obsolete in some airports and require modernization.[72] The terminal buildings after remodeling will contribute to actualizing Government's vision of making the airport management of international repute for enhanced internal security.

105.   Additional capacity is prerequisite in any remodeling exercise. It was further discovered that the renovation and upgrade projects are basically on the redesign of the exterior facades and construction of the interior of the buildings to give a modern look, among others. According to aviation experts, aviation road map, is designed to revolutionalise the aviation industry and increase revenue derivable from it by 300 per cent.[73] This entails institutionalising world class safety and security standards, through institutional reforms, infrastructure development and development of airport cities (aeropolis) that would transform airports into major employment, shopping, trading, business, leisure and cargo business destinations.[74] From the foregoing, airport remodeling holds prospects for revitalized airport management and enhanced internal security.

AIRPORT EXPANSION

106.   Airport expansion is increasing size and capability of airports. A country's national airline should be in talks with private investors about setting up a robust national flag-carrier as it plans to expand airport infrastructure for enhanced airport management and internal security. It is imperative to rebuilding old airport terminals and constructing new ones as demand for air travel swells.[75] According to aviation experts, it is equally imperative that government could set up plans to start a robust national carrier within the same period to tap into growth of airport management.[76] The national carrier will be commercially run in accordance with ICAO SARPs.

107.   A country with a big economy, could sign over $500m loan agreement with the Export-Import Bank of China or the likes to fund the new airports terminals in her major cities. [77] The Government could be totally changing the face of key airports and studying the possibility of attracting private capital to take part in the expansion agenda. The government could also build some cargo airports across the country for export of perishable agricultural produce such as pineapples, mangoes and tomatoes among others. Thus, airport expansion is a prospect for airport management and internal security.

NATIONAL IDENTITY MANAGEMENT COMMISSION

108.   The National Identity Management Commission (NIMC) could be pushing for the use of the new national e-ID card as a valid travel document which will serve as an alternative to the international passport for certain types of travels. The new national e-ID card issued would be a bona fide machine readable travel document (MRTD) recognized by ICAO and NIMC.[78] Its development was as a result of NIMC's conformance to the ICAO document 9303 parts 1 and 2 for enhanced airport management. The NIMC e-ID card, if adopted will make documentation and travelling easier as the loss of the identity card would not impair the information therein as it would not be accessed by other people.

109. The ICAO applet is active at the time one picks up his e-ID card, or the citizen may wish to activate it to make travelling easier for him or her. The first generation of cards have been the smartcard chip, but future generations will be dual-interface (chip and contactless) for a truly robust solution thereby enhancing airport management. It is therefore expected that the introduction of e-ID card would revitalized airport management in accordance with ICAO SARPs. These prospects if backed with the appropriate strategies would strengthen airport management thereby improving internal security.

SUMMARY OF RESEARCH FINDINGS

110. In addition to data already analysed in this chapter, **Enclosure** 2 contain detailed inferential statistical data analysis using qualitative and descriptive methods of data presentation. Based on these analyses, the research found out that:

    a.   There is a strong and positive liner relationship between Airport Management and Internal Security.

    b.   The state of policy framework, critical support infrastructure, skilled manpower, airport security situation and funding are issues involved in airport management and internal security.

    c.   The promotion of airport management is contributing to increased revenue generation, growth in SMEs, employment generation, promoting import and export businesses.

d. Inadequate policy framework, infrastructure deficiency, insufficient manpower, insufficiency of airport security and inappropriate budgetary allocation are challenges militating against airport management and internal security.

e. The aviation intervention fund, airport remodeling, airport expansion and NIMC e-ID card hold prospects for airport management and internal security.

CHAPTER 4

STRATEGIES TO MITIGATE THE CHALLENGES TO AIRPORT MANAGEMENT IN ORDER TO ENHANCE INTERNAL SECURITY

111.   This chapter will proffer some strategies to mitigate the challenges to airport management for enhanced internal security. These strategies include formulation of policy to promote synergy and improve inter-agency cooperation, establishment of infrastructure concession agency, provision of skilled manpower, establishment of airport security force (ASF) (Code named 'Blue Force') and increase budgetary allocation. The Chapter will also present the implementation plan for these strategies.

FORMULATION OF POLICY TO PROMOTE SYNERGY AND IMPROVE INTER-AGENCY COOPERATION

112.   Airport management is a complementary system, which requires the cooperation and collaboration of all stakeholders at the

airport. The Ministry of Aviation's effort at enforcing effective airport management has been hampered by lack of clearly defined policy to promote synergy and improve inter-agency cooperation at the airports. This has led to poor coordination, inadequate inter-agency cooperation and inter-service rivalry. There is also inadequate integrated intelligence and communication network between the security agencies at the airport and aviation security personnel. These have posed hindrances to inter-agency synergy and interoperability, which militate against effective airport management and internal security.

113. Pursuance to this, the Ministry of aviation in conjunction with the stakeholders, could bring to fruition the formulation of policy to accelerate synergy and improve inter-agency cooperation in all the airports. This would strengthen inter-agency partnership in crime prevention and control for enhanced airport management and internal security. This partnership could involve the military, paramilitary agencies and aviation security. The measure would thus motivate security agencies and airport community to partner with the proposed ASF in curbing crime and terror attack for enhanced airport management and internal security.

ESTABLISHMENT OF INFRASTRUCTURE CONCESSION AGENCY

114. The deplorable state of perimeter fencing, access roads, lack of watch towers around the airports among other infrastructure decay is largely due to paucity of fund. This can be addressed by the Ministry of aviation going into partnership with the private sector on infrastructure development. This is in line with global best practice on infrastructure development among others. Such a concession, operated under the auspices of Build, Operate and Transfer (BOT) arrangement, which would ensure a robust, efficient and equitable process in addressing the critical infrastructure deficits and hence facilitates sustainable management.

115.   Pursuance to this, the Ministry of aviation in conjunction with the Federal Ministry of works, could bring to fruition the establishment of an Infrastructure Concession Agency (ICA) to accelerate development of critical support infrastructure through private sector funding. The thrust of the proposed Agency would be to create new infrastructure as well as improve on existing ones in accordance with the established standards. The Agency's priority areas could include aggressive erection of perimeter fencing mounted with electric barb wires with CCTV coverage, building of watch towers, observation posts, improvement of airport facilities, repositioning the aviation industry to better meet the need of travelers for safe and efficient air operations. This could consequently boost the infrastructure profile of aviation sector for enhanced airport management and internal security.

PROVISION OF ADEQUATE SKILLED MANPOWER

116.   The aviation sector will require adequate skilled manpower and platforms to ameliorate the challenges of unskilled manpower for enhanced airport management and internal security. Accordingly, 2 measures are involved, namely, training of existing aviation security staff could be undertaking or recruitment of personnel with security base skills. This strategy would be to address inadequate policing of the entire airport environment, reinvigorate the implementation of observation posts and watch towers around the airports. In the medium term, to boost the manpower and strengthen the security architecture of all airports there is the need to establish a dedicated ASF, financed and equipped through appropriate trust funds for enhanced airport management and internal security.

117.   There are several options for financing the proposed ASF equipment and services, one of which is the use of a consortium of banks, which will later be reimbursed from the aviation sector's earnings from airport management. Other options include be the use of National Petroleum Corporation Trust Fund to finance the propose ASF. Drawing from the excess crude savings or from the foreign reserve are other options. The implementation of the ASF is to be phase into short, medium and long terms, covering a period of 3 years. The short term would be for the recruitment and orientation of personnel of the proposed ASF from the armed forces, police and paramilitary forces. This period would also be used for the provisioning of equipment and platforms for use of the force. The medium term will be acquisition of needed hardware and heavy surveillance and platforms, while in the long term, efforts would focus on indigenization of maintenance of the surveillance equipment and platforms.

ESTABLISHMENT OF AIRPORT SECURITY FORCE (BLUE FORCE)

118.   The objective of the proposed ASF is to provide enabling environment for improved operational effectiveness of airport management and internal security. The establishment authority will provide the policy guideline for the conduct of operations and training of the

proposed Force. The organogram of the proposed force structure is at **Appendix** 4. The ASF is to be commanded by an officer of the rank of Air Cdre. The decision for the suggestion of a proposed ASF came in mind following the spate of armed robbery attacks at the airports and recently threats of terror attacks. It could be recalled that, since 9/11, some countries have been witnessing various forms of terrorist attacks against citizens, corporate organizations and government institutions and facilities among others. These attacks came in varied forms ranging from a variety of improvised explosive devices (IEDs) and vehicle borne explosives (VIEDs) which impact negatively on internal security.

119. Positioning of the proposed ASF and boosting its manpower and equipment will require huge financial commitments. This will entail synergy of efforts that incorporates the financial power of the aviation industry and government statutory allocations. The Office of the National Security Adviser (ONSA) could press for a legislation that will create the 'Force' and provide dedicated fund for the management and training of skilled manpower. Furthermore, the ONSA could lobby the National Assembly (NASS) to allocate at least 0.5 per cent of the nation's GDP to the management of proposed ASF funding for enhanced airport management and internal security.

INCREASED BUDGETRY ALLOCATION

120. The government needs to diversify its sources of funding for the aviation industry. Apart from regular annual fiscal allocations, a more comprehensive mechanism to fund the proposed ASF could be developed to speed up the establishment of the Force following growing concern for safe and efficient conduct of air operations and safety of passengers. In this regard, the government could sponsor a bill to NASS for the creation of ASF for enhanced airport management and internal security. The fund would enable the ONSA to provide adequate airport security structure for the aviation sector for enhanced airport management and internal security.

121. Furthermore, the ONSA could in collaboration with the Ministry of aviation enact a legislation compelling other agencies at the airports to be subordinated to ASF as far as entire security architecture of airport and its environment is concern. This will enable the Force to carry out its assigned role of ensuring the safety of the passengers, aircraft and airport for enhanced airport management and internal security. These measures could boost fund generation by providing considerable level of security, build confidence in the minds of passengers, airliners, staff and businessmen thereby contributing further to revenue generation for enhanced airport management and internal security.

IMPLIMENTATION PLAN

122. In order to ensure the implementation of the strategies proffered to mitigate the challenges of airport management for enhanced internal security, there is the need to articulate the implementation plan. Consequently, a phased implementation plan which could be carried out in 3 phases is hereby proposed. The phases of the Implementation Plan which is at **Appendix** 5 are discussed in subsequent paragraphs.

123.   Phase 1: Short Term (0 – 6 Months). Phase 1 is the preparatory phase and would involve consultation with relevant stakeholders, preparation of draft Executive Bills for the NASS and setting up of committees to commence implementation of the various aspects of the strategies. This phase would also entail conducting feasibility studies and assessment of the aviation sector.

124.   Phase 2: Medium Term (6 – 12 Months). Phase 2 is the execution phase and would involve deliberations among stakeholders, hearing and passing into law of the executive bills before the NASS. These laws will then be sent to the ONSA for the NSA assent. This phase will also see to the appropriate appropriation of budgetary allocations to airport management for enhanced internal security.

125.   Phase 3: Long Term (12 Months and above). Phase 3 is the consolidation and execution phase. In recognition of the imperatives of sustainability, it would involve the completion of existing plans, evaluation and re-evaluation of already existing plans to serve as feedback for possible adjustment.

126.   Implementation Coordination. To ensure effective implementation of the proffered strategies, relevant ministries, departments and agencies as well as ONSA will be involved in the coordination of the plan.

CHAPTER 5

CONCLUSION AND RECOMMENDATIONS

127. This chapter comprises the conclusion and recommendations sections. It presents a synopsis of the study and recommendations for improving airport management for enhanced internal security.

CONCLUSION

128. There is a strong positive correlation between airport management and internal security. Airports are widely built in almost all the states of the federation to showcase the immense potential of the country and to enhance the movement of people from one state or country to another. However, over the years, these airports were built without having in view the immense economic potentials they have to better the economic well-being of the people. Similarly also, without projecting that the number of airport users, volume of traffic and other associated businesses at the airports would increase beyond measure, hence renovation and expansion is imperative. A detailed investigation of the subject revealed that policy framework, airport support infrastructure, skilled manpower development, airport security and funding are issues involved in airport management and internal security. It was discovered that airport management is contributing to the economic development through increased revenue generation to the aviation sector, government, organized private sectors as well as individuals involved in the management of businesses at the airports. The other areas of contribution are evident in the growth in number of SMEs and creation of employments at the airport to enhance socio-economic well-being of the citizens.

129. Among several other challenges, inadequate policy framework is a major challenge militating against airport management and internal security. Others included infrastructure deficits; the study identified the deplorable state of perimeter fencing and access roads at the airports as posing the most daunting challenge to airport management and internal security. Also, of serious concern among the identified challenges is inadequate skilled manpower to handle security and some of the highly technical equipment due to inadequate training and orientation. In furtherance to the identified challenges is the state of insecurity at the airports occasioned by rising crime rate mostly targeted against travelers especially during festive periods and threats of attacks at the airports due to rising cases of terrorist activities within the world. The other challenge militating against airport management and internal security was identified to include inappropriate budgetary allocation to carter for most of the identified challenges in areas of provisioning of perimeter fence, building of watch towers, CCTV and purchase of modern security hardware among others. This was found to be partly due to the capital intensive nature of some of the identified challenges.

130.   There is also the challenge of establishing airport security force whose responsibility would be to ensure safe and efficient conduct of air operations and security of airports. Additionally, due to other competing demands and paucity of funds, there has been funding gap for aviation sector development. The last of these challenges is the level of touting and rowdiness due to ineffective control of movement of passengers and non-passengers within the terminal buildings at the airports.

131.   Despite the identified challenges, there are some prospects of airport management and internal security. These include aviation intervention fund and airport remodeling. Others are airport expansion and National Identity Management Commission in aviation to ease physical identification by airport management at the check-in counters hold bright prospects for airport management and internal security. In order to address the identified challenges, it was proffered that the Federal Government could formulate policy to promote synergy and improve inter-agency cooperation. Others are to create an ICA to improve infrastructure state. The provision of adequate manpower and equipment to handle some of the identified challenges is necessary to build a society free from crimes. In the same vein, the Federal Government could embark on intensive sensitization and establishment of Airport Security Force (Blue Force).

132.   In order to create conducive environment for airport management and internal security devoid of crimes and threats of terror attack, the Federal Government could increase budgetary allocation

to the Ministry of aviation to handle some of the identified deficit in airport management for enhanced internal security. This will enable the propose Force to carry out its assigned role of ensuring the safety of the passengers, aircraft and airports for enhanced airport management and internal security. These measures could boost fund generation and contribute further to internal security. In general, the establishment of the Force could improve country's image abroad and earn her the respect of other nations/countries for operating safe and efficient airport management for enhanced internal security.

RECOMMENDATIONS

133.   It is recommended that the Federal Government should:

a.   Formulate a policy to promote synergy and improve inter-agency corporation at the airports.

b.   Create Infrastructure concession Agency to address the perimeter fencing, watch towers, road infrastructure deficit at the airports.

c.   Partner with relevant agencies to provide adequate skilled manpower and equipment to boost airport management and internal security.

d.   Create intensive sensitization and establishment of Airport Security Force to ensure safe, efficient and conducive environment of air operations.

e.   Increase budgetary allocation to boost funding of airport management and internal security.

f. Create the Headquarters of Airport Security Force at the Presidency.

BIBLIOGRAPHY

BOOKS

Clark JR, **Intelligence and National Security: A Reference Handbook** (Connecticut; Greenwood Publishing Group, 2007).

Nnoli O, **National Security in Africa; A Radical New Perspective,** (Enugu: SNAAP Press Ltd, 2006).

McNamara R, **The Essence of Security**, (New York: Harper and Row, 1968).

Bartholomew E, **Airport and Aviation Security**, (Aviation Infrastructure Protection, 2009).

Jenkins B, **The Breach of Security of San Jose Airport Raises Broader Issues**, 13 May 2014.

Nwoke CN, **Cotemporary Challenges in Nigeria, Africa and the World**, 2014.

PERIODICALS/JOURNALS

Bolaji O, **The Military in Airport Security: The Airman, The Nigerian Air Force Journal**, Vol. 9, No. 4, 2005.

Demuren H, "Nigeria's Aviation Industry Has Moved Tremendously", **Aviation and Allied Business Update**, March 2007.

Civil Aviation Authority Journal," Airspace for Tomorrow", (United Kingdom), October 2009.

Dike P, **Nigeria Accident Investigation, Bureau**, 8 June 2012.

Obilana A, "Security and Safety in Civil Aviation Emerging Threats and Challenges for Stakeholders", **Aviation and Allied Business Update**, November (2004).

Yilwa J, "New Civil Aviation Act", **Journal of Federal Ministry of Transport**, Vol. 7, No. 2 (2007).

OFFICIAL PUBLICATIONS

Airworthiness Standards, Nigerian Civil Aviation Authority, CARs/ ICAO **Publications.**

Aviation Reform in Nigeria- **African Aviation**, February 2006.

NEWSPAPER/MAGAZINES

Akpan I, "Nigerian Aviation Industry 1960 – 2009", **Leadership Newpaper,** (Abuja), 2 October 2009.

Amaefule E, "Why Nigeria Recorded Plan Crashes at Weekends", **The Punch Newspaper**, (Ibadan), 11 December 2006.

Shadare W, Strengthening Civil Aviation through Efficiency Safety Regulation", **Guardian Newspaper**, (Lagos), 5 February 2010.

INTERNET/ELECTRONIC MEDIA

Avjobs.com, **History of Aviation,** <http://www.avjobs.com/history/index.asp.html> access 18 Nov 14 by 1300hrs.

History of ICAO, <http://www.icao.int /icap/en/hist/history02.html> accessed 1 Oct 14 by 1200hrs.

South African Power Flying Association, **The History of Aviation in South Africa**, <http.sapfa.org.za/history/history2/php> accessed 3 October 2014 by 1500

Jake Okechukwu, "Aviation Reforms in Nigeria," <http:/www.academia.edu/aviation- reforms. Html>, accessed 29 Dec 14.

EUROCONTROL – Total Airport Management, <http:/www.eurocontrol. int/proj_care_information.com. html>. Accessed 6 Dec 14.

Airport Management Career Overview, <http://www.avjobs. com. html> accessed 14 Dec 14.

Airport Management Definition, <http:/www.answers.com/airport_manag ement.html>, accessed 15 Dec 14..

Walter Lippmann, Concept of National Security, <http:/www.centaur.reading.ac.uk/Patrick__porter_centaur.com.html>, accessed 16 Dec 14.

M Jenkins, **Airport Raises Border Issues,** 13 May 14, <http://www.thecable.ng/security-and-national-development|TheCable.html>, accessed 25 Nov14 by 1800hrs.

History of Aviation, <http://www.ICAO.Int/icap/en/hist/history.02.html>, accessed 2 Jan 15.

NCAA Regulation, Nigeria Civil Aviation Authority, <http://www.ncaa.gov.ng/regulations/ncaa.regulations/html> accessed 6 Jan 15.

Aviation Portal Turning Point for Nigeria's Air Passengers, <http://www.allafrica.com/stories.html>, 19 Dec 14. Accessed 8 Jan 15.

The Punch, "Stowaway Boy thought Arik plane was US-Bond", <http://www.punching.com/stowaway-boy-benin-Lagos.htm>, 26 Aug 13, accessed on 8 Jan 15.

Northwest Airlines Flight 253, <http://www.nytimes.com/2009/us/26plane.html>, 25 Dec 09, accessed 8 Jan 15.

allafrica.com: Nigeria: Re – the Many Gods of Aviation, <http://www.allafrica.com/stories/2013.html>, 20 Oct 13, accessed 9 Jan 15.

Bank of Industry, Power and Aviation Fund, <http:www.boinigeria.com/power-and-aviation-fund/info@boinigeria.com. html>, 6 Jun 14. Accessed 9 Jan 15.

Nigerian Airport, FAAN Internally Generated Revenue, <http://www.vanguardngr.com/nigerian-airport.com.html>, 14 Dec 10-15 Dec 14, accessed 9 Jan 15.

NCAA Regulation: Nigeria Civil Aviation Authority, <http://www.ncaa.gov.ng/regulations/ncaa.com.html>, 2006, accessed 10 Jan 15.

UNPUBLISHED MATERIALS

Enechukwu C, "Aviation Management and National Security", a paper presented at the Aviation Seminar, Nigerian Civil Aviation Technology, Zaria, Jun 06.

Auyo I, "Points Way Forward for Air Traffic Management", a paper presented at an International Conference at Lagos Airport Hotel, Ikeja, 21 Jan 14.

Aisuebeogun R, "Financing Airport Expansion and Development in Africa: The FAAN Experience", a paper presented at the Workshop Expo 2009, Lagos, Oct 09.

UNSTRUCTURED INTERVIEW

Dunoma S, Managing Director and Chief Executive Officer, Federal Airport Authority of Nigeria, interviewed on "Airport Management and National security in Nigeria", 30 Dec 14.

Mohammed KY, Chief of Staff to the Managing Director and Chief Executive Officer, Federal Airport Authority of Nigeria, interviewed on "Airport Management and National Security in Nigeria", 30 Dec 14.

Abdusalam I, Managing Director and Chief Executive Officer, Nigerian Airspace Management Agency, interviewed on "Airport Management and National Security in Nigeria", 30 Dec 14.

Pwajok ML, Special Adviser to Managing Director and Chief Executive Officer, Airspace Management agency, interviewed on "Airport Management and National Security in Nigeria, 30 Dec 14.

Mark N, Managing Director DAAN Aviation, Lagos, interviewed on "Airport Management and National Security in Nigeria", 31 Dec 14.

Dueuk C, Chief Executive Officer Blue Lodge, Murtala Mohammed International Airport, interviewed on "Airport Management and National security in Nigeria", 31 Dec 14.

Korie C, Assistant Comptroller Immigration, Murtala Mohammed International Airport, Lagos, interview on "Airport Management and National Security in Nigeria", on 1 Jan 14.

Onaroh A, Chairman Aviation Security, Federal Airport Authority of Nigeria, interviewed on "Airport Management and National Security in Nigeria, 1 Jan 05.

LIST OF APPENDICES AND ENCLOSURE

APPENDICES

1. List of Airports in Nigeria Grouped by Type and Sorted by Location.

2. A Copy of the Questionnaire

3. List of Secondary Sources of Data.

4. Organogram of the Proposed 'Force' Structure.

5. Implementation Plan.

ENCLOSURE

1. Distribution Strategy of the questionnaire.

ENDNOTES

1. Avjobs.com, **History of Aviation,** <http://www.avjobs.com/history/ index.asp.html>.

2. **Ibid.**

3. History of ICAO, <http://www.icao.int /icap/en/hist/history02.html> accessed.

4. **Ibid.**

5. Airspace for Tomorrow, Civil Aviation Authority Journal, (United Kingdom). p15.

6. South African Power Flying Association, **The History of Aviation in South Africa,** <http.sapfa.org.za/history/history2/php> .

7. **Ibid.**

8. Report of the Panel on Activities of Civil Aviation Department, "History of Aviation in Nigeria", (Lagos: Federal Government Press, 1985), p.13.

9. HO Demuren, "**The Role of Regulatory Bodies in Aviation**" Presentation at key to Africa Aviation Conference, Abuja, 19 – 21 September 2006.

10. Jake Okechukwu, "Aviation Reforms in Nigeria," <http:/www. academia.edu/aviation- reforms. Html> .

11. **Ibid**.

12. Essien, "Introduction to Research Methodology".

13. HR Bernard, "Social Research Methods, Qualitative and Quantitative Approaches",

14. EUROCONTROL –Total Airport Management, <u>http:/www. eurocontrol.int/proj_care_information.com. html</u>. .

15. Airport Management Career Overview, <http://www.avjobs. com.html>.

16. Airport Management Definition, <http:/www.answers.com/airport_manag ement.html>.

17. JR Clark, Intelligence and National Security: A Reference Handbook (Connecticut; Greenwood Publishing Group, 2007). p. 3.

18. Walter Lippmann, Concept of National Security, <http:/www. centaur.reading.ac.uk/Patrick__porter_centaur.com.html>.

19. O Nnoli, **National Security in Africa: A Radical New Perspective** (Enugu: PACREP, 2006), p. 6.

20. R McNamara, **The Essence of Security,** (New York: Harper and Row, 1968), pp. 33-36.

21. **Ibid**.

22. **Ibid**.

23. M Jenkins, **Airport Raises Border Issues,** 13 May 14, <http://www. thecable.ng/security-and-national-development|TheCable. html>.

24. I Akpan, "**Nigerian Aviation Industry:**" Roles of Aviation Industry in Nigeria1960 – 2009. Paper presented at Aviation seminar in Lagos, 2009.

25. **Ibid.**

26. Bartholomew Elias, Airport and Aviation Security (Aviation Infrastructure Protection, 2009), p. 118.

27. HO Demuren, "The Roles of Regulatory Bodies in Aviation", A Paper Presented at key to African Aviation Conference, Abuja, 19-21 Sep 06.

28. **Ibid.**

29. C Enechukwu, "Aviation Management and National Security" (Unpublished).

30. **Ibid.**

31. **Ibid.**

32. O Amu, "Terrorism and Airport Security in Nigeria: An Appraisal".

33. A Bankole, "Aviation Safety and Security In Nigeria: An Appraisal".

34. **Ibid.**

35. **Ibid.**

36. Ludwig von Bertalanffy, General System Theory, 1968. p.1.

37. **Ibid.**

38. Federal Aviation Administration, <http://www.faa.gov.com.
html>.

39. **Ibid.**

40. **Ibid.**

41. **Ibid.**

42. History of Aviation, <http://www.ICAO.Int/icap/en/hist/histo-
ry.02. html>.

43. H Demuren, "**The Role of Regulatory Bodies in Aviation**",
Presentation at key to African Aviation Conference, Abuja, 19-21
Sep 06.

44. **Nigeria Civil Aviation policy**, 2006.

45. ICAO, "**The Management of Airspace," Op. Cit**.

46. **Ibid.**

47. **Nigeria Civil Aviation policy**, 2006. **Op. Cit**.

48. **Nigerian Accident Investigation, Bureau**, 8 Jun 12, p. 8.

49. NCAA Regulation, Nigeria Civil Aviation Authority, <http://
www.ncaa.gov.ng/regulations/ncaa.regulations/html>.

50. Aviation Portal Turning Point for Air Passengers, <http://www.
allafrica.com/stories.html>.

51. Airport Security Committee, "Audit Report of MMIA, "2013.

52. B Jenkins, The Breach of Security of San Joses: Airport Raises
Broader issues, 4 May p.5.

53. A Obilana, "**Security and Safety in Civil Aviation: Emerging Threats and Challenges for Stakeholders. "Aviation and Allied Business Update**, 2004, p.6.

54. **Ibid**.

55. Northwest Airlines Flight 253, <http://www.nytimes.com/2009/12/26/us/26 plane.html? r=0>, 25 Dec 09.

56. allafrica.com: Re – the Many Gods of Aviation, <http://www.allafrica.com/stories/2013.html>, 20 Oct 13.

57. Bank of Industry, Power and Aviation Fund, <http:www.boinigeria.com/power-and-aviation-fund/info@boinigeria.com. html>.

58. Airport, FAAN Internally Generated Revenue, http://www.vanguardngr.com/nigerian-airport.com.html>.

59. C Dueck, CEO blue Lodge MMIA, Lagos (unstructured interview), 29 Dec 14.

60. **Op Cit**

61. Nigeria Airports, FAAN, **Op. Cit.**

62. Engr S Dunoma, MD FAAN Nigeria (unstructured interview), 20 Dec 14.

63. **Ibid**.

64. NCAA Regulation: Nigeria Civil Aviation Authority, <http://www.ncaa.gov.ng/regulations/ncaa.com.html>, 2006.

65. Yusuf Mohammed, Chief of Staff MD FAAN (unstructured interview), 20 Dec 14.

66. **Ibid**.

67. Matthew Lawrence, SA-MD/CEO Nigeria Airspace Management Agency (NAMA) (Unstructured interview), 20 Dec 14.

68. BM Jenkins. The Breach of Security at San Jose's: Airport Raises Broader Issues, 13 May 14, p.5.

69. **Ibid.**

70. Matthew Lawrence, **Op. Cit.**

71. Yusuf Mohammed, **Op. Cit.**

72. **Ibid.**

73. Airport Remodeling Growing Prospects of an unfinished surgery, <http://www.vanguardngr.com/2013/02/>.

74. **Ibid.**

75. Aviation Expansion <http://www.bloomberg.com/news/articles/2014-09-29/>

76. **Ibid.**

77. **Ibid.**

78. T Durodola, **NIMC Pushes for Adoption of National ID Card as Valid Travel Document**, <http://sunnewsonline.com/new/?p=84865>.